# Big Cats
# Past and Present

MARIANNE JOHNSTON

The Rosen Publishing Group's
## PowerKids Press™
New York

Published in 2000 by The Rosen Publishing Group, Inc.
29 East 21st Street, New York, NY 10010

First Edition

Book Design: Michael de Guzman, Resa Listort, Danielle Primiceri

Photo Credits: p. 3 © Digital Stock; p. 4 © Digital Stock and © Dr. Adrian Lister; p. 6 © E. R. Degginger and © Breck P. Kent/Animals Animals; p. 8 © Digital Stock and © Tom McHugh/Cal. Acad. of Sciences; p. 11 © Tom McHugh/Cal. Acad. of Sciences; p. 12 © John Pontier/Animals Animals; p. 15 © Dr. Adrian Lister; p. 16 © Manoj Shah/Tony Stone Worldwide and © Gerard Lacz/Animals Animals; p. 19 © Daniel J. Cox/Tony Stone Worldwide; pp. 20, 21 © Digital Stock.

Johnston, Marianne.
    Big cats past and present / by Marianne Johnston.—1st ed.
        p.    cm. — (Prehistoric animals and their modern-day relatives)
    Includes index.
    Summary: Describes the prehistoric ancestors, evolution, and modern-day members of the cat family.
    ISBN 0-8239-5203-7 (lib. bdg.)
    1. Felidae, Fossil—Juvenile literature. 2. Felidae—Juvenile literature. [1. Felidae. 2. Prehistoric animals. 3. Cats.] I. Title.
II. Series: Johnston, Marianne. Prehistoric animals and their modern-day relatives.
QE882.C15J64 1998
569'.75—dc21
                    98-46360
                    CIP

Manufactured in the United States of America                    AC

# CONTENTS

# BIG CATS

Can you picture a huge cat with long teeth sticking out of its mouth, slinking through your backyard? If you had been alive 10,000 years ago, you might have seen just that. Long ago, these saber-toothed cats walked Earth. Today, saber-toothed cats are **extinct**.

Only six kinds of big cats still exist in the entire world. All six of them are distant relatives of the saber-toothed cat.

No one knows exactly why saber-toothed cats became extinct. We do know a lot about what they were like while they were alive.

*Saber-toothed cats such as this one roamed Earth many years ago.*

What we know about **prehistoric** cats comes from **fossils**. Fossils are the **remains** of bones and teeth from plants and animals that have died. Fossils tell us a lot about what early cats were like. We can use fossils to figure out how early cats are related to modern-day cats.

Like most living things, cats have gone through **evolution**. Evolution is the slow change and development that most plants and animals go through over millions of years.

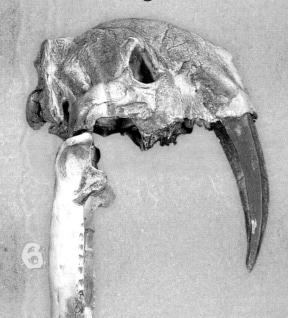

*These skeletons of prehistoric cats show us how their bodies were shaped. Look at those giant teeth!* ▶

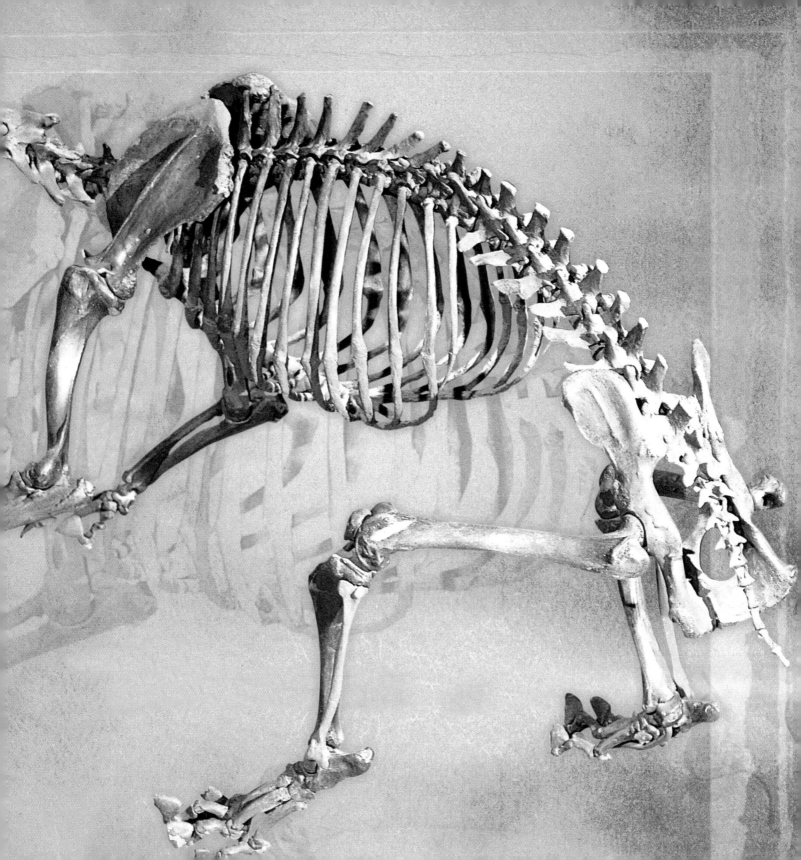

# THE FIRST CATS

The first cat-like animal that we know of lived about 30 million years ago. Fossils found in France show that this ancient cat had long legs and was just a little bigger than a large house cat is today.

About 20 million years ago, two kinds of cats developed. One kind was the saber-toothed cat. The other kind was called the true cat. Modern-day cats developed from the true cat. Saber-toothed cats and modern-day cats are related to a common **ancestor**.

*Though this kitten and this saber-toothed cat look very different, they came from the same ancestor.*

# SABER-TOOTHED CATS

Maybe you've heard of "saber-toothed tigers." They're the same as saber-toothed cats. In fact, saber-toothed cats is the correct name for these prehistoric animals.

Saber-toothed cats had long, sharp teeth called **canines**. These teeth allowed the cat to bite through the flesh of its **prey**. One saber-toothed cat, called **Homotherium,** had large, curved canines shaped like the letter C.

Several kinds of powerful saber-toothed cats once lived all around the world, in places including Africa, Europe, and North and South America.

*A saber-toothed cat would kill its prey by biting the prey's flesh with long canine teeth. Then the saber-toothed cat would wait for the animal to bleed to death.*

HUMAN TOOTH

SMILODON TOOTH

# SMILODON

The most well known saber-toothed cat was **Smilodon,** which once roamed through North and South America.

Smilodon often grew to be four feet long. Smilodon had two sharp canine teeth in the front of its mouth that were each seven inches long. The longest teeth in a grown-up human's mouth are usually no longer than half an inch!

Smilodon had very strong front legs. Powerful claws allowed Smilodon to hold on to its prey as it bit the prey's flesh with long teeth.

*The Smilodon's huge canine tooth (left) makes a human tooth (right) look tiny!*

# SABER-TOOTHED CATS IN AMERICA

North American saber-toothed cats probably hunted bison and perhaps even young **mammoths**. Smilodon lived in **prides**, or groups, just like modern-day lions do. And the loud roar of Smilodon would probably sound just like the roar of lions today.

Scientists continue to find information about cats of long ago. In fact, fossils from thousands of saber-toothed cats have been found at the Rancho La Brea tar pits in downtown Los Angeles, California.

*More than 2,000 Smilodon skeletons have been found in the La Brea tar pits.*

# MODERN CATS

While the saber-toothed cats were developing, so were their cousins, the true cats. Six **species** of big cats developed from the true cats: lions, tigers, leopards, jaguars, pumas, and cheetahs.

Each of these species of cats has **characteristics** that make it special. Lions are the only big cats who live in family groups, called prides. Cheetahs are known for their incredible speed. Jaguars and leopards use their spotted coats to hide from **predators**. Tigers are the biggest of the big cats, and pumas, with their beautiful, tan coats, are the only big cats left in North America.

*The different types of cats also developed different styles of hunting. For example, tigers hunt alone, while lions hunt in groups.*

17

The United States is home to the puma, which is often called the mountain lion. These large cats once roamed all around North America. Now they live mostly in the western part of the United States and South America.

The rain forests of South America are home to the secretive jaguar. This spotted cat has the strongest bite of all modern big cats. Sadly, jaguars are **endangered** today. Many people around the world are trying to save the rain forests where the jaguars live. If we save the forests in which the jaguars live, we can save the jaguars.

*All big cats, such as the puma, are in danger today. This is because people are using more and more land that the cats live on to build towns and cities.*

# HOUSE CATS

About one million years ago, another type of cat evolved. This type was called **Felis sylvestris**. These cats were much smaller than the big cats that had evolved before them. But they came from the same ancestor.

Even though *Felis sylvestris* was smaller, it still looked very much like the big cats. And it lived, ate, and hunted much like the big cats. Today's pet cats are the modern-day relatives of *Felis sylvestris*.

*Can you believe that this tiny kitten is a relative of the giant, prehistoric Smilodon? Well, it is!*

# CATS OF YESTERDAY AND TODAY

The cats of the past had many of the same characteristics as today's cats. The size and shape of prehistoric cats stayed about the same as they evolved into modern-day big cats. Also, both prehistoric and modern cats have large canine teeth used for killing their prey. Even though the teeth of today's cats are smaller than those of prehistoric cats, the fact that they both have these special teeth shows a connection between them. Looking at today's cats, big and small, helps us learn more about their prehistoric relatives.

## WEB SITES:

http://www.lam.mus.ca.us/cats/
http://www.all90.com/users/sgprice
/wildcats/index.htm

# GLOSSARY

**ancestor** (AN-ses-ter)  A creature from which others evolve.

**canine** (KAY-nyn)   A certain tooth found in animals and located on the side of the mouth toward the front.

**characteristic** (KAR-ek-ter-IS-tik)  A feature that makes something or someone special.

**endangered** (en-DAYN-jerd)   Something that is in danger of no longer existing.

**evolution** (eh-vuh-LOO-shun)  A slow process of change and development that living things go through over many, many years.

**extinct** (ek-STINKT)  When something no longer exists.

*Felis sylvestris* (FEE-lis sil-VES-tris)  The scientific name for a house cat.

**fossil** (FAH-sul)  The hardened remains of plants and animals that have been dead for a long time.

**Homotherium** (hoh-moh-THEER-ee-um)  A saber-toothed cat that had canines shaped like the letter C.

**mammoth** (MA-muth)  A prehistoric close relative of the elephant that lived until 10,000 years ago.

**predator** (PREH-duh-ter)  An animal that eats other animals for food.

**prehistoric** (pree-his-TOR-ik)  Happening before recorded history.

**prey** (PRAY)  An animal that is eaten by another animal for food.

**pride** (PRYD)  A group of lions that live together.

**remains** (re-MAYNZ)  What's left of a plant or animal after it has died.

**Smilodon** (SMY-loh-dahn)  One of the most well-known kinds of saber-toothed cats.

**species** (SPEE-sheez)  A group of animals that are very much alike.

# INDEX